Bread Machine Recipes

Easy To Follow Steps For Delicious Bread In No Time

Sherry S. Williams

Bread Machine Recipes: Easy To Follow Steps For Delicious Bread In No Time

Copyright © 2018 - All rights reserved. No part of this book may be reproduced in any form or by any means without permission in writing from the publisher, SSW Publishing. Please read the full disclaimer at the end of this book.

Table of Contents

1 - Introduction

Have you always been fascinated by the process of bread making? Doing it the usual way is fulfilling and for some, therapeutic, but can also be time-consuming. Before you can even start baking, you have to ensure that you have kneaded the dough properly and have given it enough time to rise and rest.

The introduction of bread makers or bread machines made it possible for more people to bake bread at home. This is done in a faster way than usual and you can easily do it even though you haven't tried doing something like this before. All you need is a handy machine, which is now available in various models, sizes, and brands. The dough will still go through the usual process of kneading, rising, and all that, but this time, you can leave the machine as it works on your bread and come back when it's done.

So how do you use a bread machine? First, place the appliance on a counter near an outlet. Do not plug it yet.

Check if the lid will open easily without hitting any other tools or cabinets in the kitchen. Remove the baking pan. Wash it with gentle soap, rinse thoroughly and let it dry before using.

1 - INTRODUCTION

Place the kneading blade to plan and set it aside. Follow the recipe for the bread you are making.

Place the baking pan in the machine, close the lid, plug it in, and choose the right settings based on the recipe you're doing.

Press the Start/Stop button to begin the bread making process.

Note that there are certain recipes wherein you'll be required to raise the lid during the process to add certain ingredients, such as fruits and nuts. There are also certain brands that have an automatic fruit and nut dispenser feature.

It is important to use the exact measurement of each ingredient in the recipe. The yeast must not come into contact with liquid during the preparation process. You must first make a small well at the center of the ingredients in the pan using your hand where you will put the yeast.

When it comes to settings, the basic types found in many bread machines include the following:

Basic or White setting lasts for 3 hours. This is used in

many recipes because it creates the best results among all the other settings.

The Whole wheat setting lasts for 3 hours and 40 minutes. The duration is longer than the basic setting because bread with more than 50 percent whole wheat flour needs longer time to rise.

The French setting lasts for 3 hours and 50 minutes. French bread has a heartier crust that needs longer time to knead, rise, and bake.

The Sweet setting lasts for 2 hours and 50 minutes. This is used for recipes with lots of proteins, fats, and sugar.

The Dough setting lasts for 1 hour and 30 minutes. This is used in preparing dough for specialty bread and rolls that you will later shape using your hands, leave to rise, and bake in an oven.

The Bake setting lasts for 1 hour and is used in making jams or dough. There are also models with the Expressbake feature that you can use in baking bread in less than an hour or 80 minutes for larger loaves.

Another button that you need to set is the crust color button. Your choice depends on your personal preference. L is for light, P is for medium, and H is for dark. The names of the settings may vary depending on the model of the machine you are using but basically have similar functions.

There are some models that have a designated setting for loaf size. In this case, you simply have to choose the size based on the recipe you're making.

Once you have placed the baking pan inside the machine with all the ingredients as per the recipe, it will go through various processes that you can see at its dedicated viewing window. Once the timer starts, the machine will knead the dough for the first 10 minutes.

The dough will rise for 20 minutes before the machine kneads it for the second time for 15 minutes. The dough will rise again for 20 minutes and excess air is punched down for 30 seconds. The dough will have 55 minutes for its final rise before it begins to bake for the next 60 minutes.

Once the process is done, all you have to do is carefully lift the pan, turn it upside down to get the bread out and leave it for a couple of minutes to cool. If the kneading blade comes out with the bread, remove it using a plastic utensil but be careful because it is also hot. After 15 minutes, you can slice the bread and serve.

The process is easy once you get the hang of it. Make sure that you read the manual that comes with the machine and start practicing the process of bread making.

2 - White Bread Recipes

Basic White Bread

To make 1 1/2-pound loaf bread, measure the ingredients into the pan in this exact order: 1 1/4 cups of water with the temperature of 80 to 90 degrees Fahrenheit, 2 tablespoons unsalted butter cut into cubes, 2 teaspoons sugar, 2 tablespoons dry skim milk powder, 1 teaspoon salt, 3 1/4 cups of bread flour, and 1 1/4 teaspoons of yeast.

Snap the bread pan inside the machine, lock the lid, and plug it in. Choose the Basic/White setting and your preferred color for the crust. Press the Start/Stop button to start the process. Once done, carefully remove the pan from the machine and allow the bread to cool before slicing.

Beer Bread

To make 1 1/2-pound loaf bread, measure the ingredients into the pan in this exact order: 1/2 cup of beer with the temperature of 80 to 90 degrees Fahrenheit, 1/2 cup of water with the temperature of 80 to 90 degrees Fahrenheit, 1/4 cup of chopped green onions, 2 teaspoons of sugar, 1 teaspoon of salt, 3 cups of bread flour, and 1 1/2 teaspoons of yeast.

Place the bread pan inside the machine, close the lid, and plug it in. Choose the Basic/White setting and your preferred color of the crust before pressing the Start/Stop button. Once it's done, carefully remove the pan and transfer the loaf to a wire rack to cool before slicing.

Swiss Cheese Bread

To make 1 1/2-pound loaf bread, measure the ingredients into the pan in this exact order: 3/4 cup of buttermilk with the temperature of 80 to 90 degrees Fahrenheit, 1/3 cup of water with the temperature of 80 to 90 degrees Fahrenheit, 3/4 cup of shredded Swiss cheese, 1 tablespoon of honey, 1 tablespoon of baking powder, 3/4 teaspoon of dried dill, 3/4 teaspoon of dried chives, 1 teaspoon of salt, 3 1/2 cups of bread flour, and 1 3/4 teaspoons of yeast.

Snap the bread pan inside the machine, lock the lid, and plug it in. Select the Basic/White setting and the crust color you prefer. Press the Start/Stop button to start the process. Open the machine and carefully remove the pan. Allow the bread to cool for at least 15 minutes before serving.

Onion Cheese Bread

To make 1 1/2-pound loaf bread, measure the ingredients into the pan in this exact order: 1/2 cup water with temperature of 80 to 90 degrees Fahrenheit, 1/3 cup of cottage cheese, 1/4 cup of shredded Swiss cheese, 3 tablespoons of grated Parmesan cheese, 2 teaspoons of unsalted butter, cut into cubes, 1 1/2 tablespoons of sugar, 1 1/4 teaspoons of salt, 2 teaspoons of minced onion, 1 tablespoon of chopped parsley, 2 3/4 cups of bread flour, and 1 1/4 teaspoons of yeast.

Snap the bread pan inside the machine, lock the lid, and plug it in. Set the machine to Basic/White and your preferred crust color. Press the Start/Stop button to start the process. Carefully lift the pan out of the machine and leave the bread to cool before slicing.

Maple Walnut Bread

To make 1 1/2-pound loaf bread, measure the ingredients into the pan in this exact order: 1 cup and 2 tablespoons of water with the temperature of 80 to 90 degrees Fahrenheit, 4 tablespoons of vegetable oil, 6 tablespoons of maple syrup, half a teaspoon of lemon extract, 1 teaspoon of salt, 1 cup of instant oatmeal, 3 1/2 cups of bread flour, and 3/4 teaspoon of yeast.

Snap the bread pan into the machine and lock the lid. Place 1/2 cup of chopped walnuts in the automatic fruit and nut dispenser. Plug the unit and select the Basic/White setting and your preferred color of the crust. Carefully get the pan out once done and transfer the loaf to a wire rack to cool.

3 - Whole Wheat Bread Recipes

Whole Wheat Bread

To make 1 1/2-pound loaf bread, measure the ingredients into the pan in this exact order: 1/2 cup of milk with the temperature of 80 to 90 degrees Fahrenheit, 1/4 cup of water with the temperature of 80 to 90 degrees Fahrenheit, 1/4 cup of small curd cottage cheese with the temperature of 80 to 90 degrees Fahrenheit, 3 tablespoons of unsalted butter cut into cubes, 3 tablespoons of honey, 1 1/2 teaspoons of salt, 1 cup of whole wheat flour, 2 1/2 cups of bread flour, and 1 3/4 teaspoons of yeast.

Snap the pan into the machine before locking the lid. Plug the machine into an outlet. Choose the Whole Wheat setting and your desired color of the crust. Press the Start/Stop button. Once done, carefully remove the pan from the unit and transfer the loaf to a wire rack to cool.

Whole Wheat Bread with Raisin

To make 1 1/2-pound loaf bread, measure the ingredients into the pan in this exact order: 1 1/4 cups of water with the temperature of 80 to 90 degrees Fahrenheit, 2 tablespoons of unsalted butter cut into cubes, 4 teaspoons of honey, 4 teaspoons of grated orange peel, 1 teaspoon of salt, 3/4 teaspoon of ground cinnamon, 1 1/4 cups of whole wheat flour, 2 cups of bread flour, 1 1/2 teaspoons of vital wheat gluten, and 2 teaspoons of yeast.

Place the pan inside the unit and close the lid. Place 1/3 cup of chopped walnuts and 1/3 cup of raisins in the automatic fruit and nut dispenser. Plug the unit and choose the Whole Wheat setting and your preferred color of the crust. Press the Start/Stop button. Once done, carefully get the pan and transfer the bread to a wire rack.

Pecan and Oatmeal Bread

To make 1 1/2-pound loaf bread, measure the ingredients into the pan in this exact order: 1 1/4 cups of water with the temperature of 80 to 90 degrees Fahrenheit, 1/4 cup of molasses, 1 tablespoon of vegetable oil, 1 1/2 teaspoons of salt, half a cup of instant oatmeal, 1 cup of whole wheat flour, 2 1/2 cups of bread flour, and 2 teaspoons of yeast. Snap the pan into the machine, lock the lid, and plug it in.

Set the unit to Whole Wheat and choose your desired color of the crust. Press the Start/Stop button. Upon hearing the "add ingredient" beep, gently lift the lid and add 1/3 cup of chopped toasted pecans and 1/2 cup of chopped dried apricots to the pan. Close the lid and the cooking process will continue. Open the lid when the cooking process is complete. Gently lift the pan and transfer the loaf to a wire rack to cool.

Caraway Rye Bread

Here are the steps to follow to make 1 1/2-pound loaf bread: Put 1 egg in the measuring cup. Make sure that it is at room temperature. Add enough water with the temperature of 80 to 90 degrees Fahrenheit to the cup to measure 1 1/4 cups along with the egg.

Place them into the bread pan and add the other ingredients in this exact order: 3 tablespoons of oil, 3 tablespoons of honey, 2 tablespoons of dry skim milk powder, 1 1/4 teaspoons of salt, 1 1/2 cups of bread flour, 1 cup of rye flour, 3/4 cup of whole wheat flour, 1 1/2 tablespoons of caraway seeds, and 1 1/4 teaspoons of yeast.

Snap the pan into the unit, lock the lid, and plug it into an outlet. Choose the right settings – Whole Wheat and your preferred crust color. Press the Start/Stop button. Lift the pan out once the timer is up. Transfer the loaf to a wire rack and allow to cool before slicing.

Whole Wheat Bread with Cranberry

To make 1 1/2-pound loaf bread, measure the ingredients into the pan in this exact order: 1 cup of water with the temperature of 80 to 90 degrees Fahrenheit, 2 tablespoons of unsalted butter cut into cubes, 4 teaspoons of honey, 1 1/2 teaspoons of grated orange peel, 1 teaspoon of salt, 1 1/4 cups of whole wheat flour, 2 cups of bread flour, 1 teaspoon of vital wheat gluten, and 2 teaspoons of yeast. Place the pan inside the machine, close the lid, and plug it in.

Choose the Whole Wheat setting and your desired crust color. Press the Start/Stop button. Once you hear the "add ingredient" beep, carefully open the lid and add 3/4 cup of dried cranberries into the pan. Close the lid and the cooking process will continue. Once done, gently remove the pan and transfer the loaf to a wire rack.

4 - Sweet Bread Recipes

Tropical Fruit Bread

Here are the steps to follow to make 1 1/2-pound loaf bread: Put 1 egg in the measuring cup. Make sure that it is at a room temperature. Add enough water with the temperature of 80 to 90 degrees Fahrenheit to the cup to measure 3/4 cup along with the egg.

Place them into the bread pan and add the other ingredients in this exact order: 1 1/2 tablespoons of dry skim milk powder, 3/4 cup of tropical fruit pieces, 1 1/2 tablespoons of unsalted butter cut into cubes, 2 teaspoons of grated fresh orange peel, 1 1/2 tablespoons of sugar, half a teaspoon of salt, 3 cups of bread flour, and 1 3/4 teaspoons of yeast.

Snap the pan into the unit and close the lid. Put half a cup of chopped macadamia nuts in the automatic fruit and nut dispenser. Plug the unit into an outlet and choose the White setting and your preferred color of the crust. Press the Start/Stop button. Once done, remove the pan and carefully transfer the loaf to a wire rack.

Choco-Hazelnut Bread

To make 1 1/2-pound loaf bread, measure the ingredients

into the pan in this exact order: 1 egg at room temperature, 1/2 cup of water with the temperature of 80 to 90 degrees Fahrenheit, 1 1/2 tablespoons of unsalted butter cut into cubes, 1/4 cup of unsweetened cocoa powder, 1/3 cup of sugar, 1/2 teaspoon salt, 2 cups of bread flour, and 1 teaspoon of yeast.

Place the pan inside the unit and lock the lid. Put 1/2 cup of skinned, chopped, and toasted hazelnuts in the automatic fruit and nut dispenser. Plug the unit into an outlet and choose the Sweet setting and your preferred color of the crust. Once done, remove the pan from the unit and transfer loaf to a wire rack.

Raisin Bread with Cinnamon

Here are the steps to follow to make 1 1/2-pound loaf bread: Put 1 egg in the measuring cup. Make sure that it is at room temperature. Add enough water with the temperature of 80 to 90 degrees Fahrenheit to the cup to measure 1 cup along with the egg.

Place them into the bread pan and add the other ingredients in this exact order: 1 1/2 tablespoons of firmly packed light brown sugar, 1 1/2 tablespoons of dry skim milk powder, 1

1/2 tablespoons of unsalted butter cut into cubes, 1 teaspoon of ground cinnamon, 1 teaspoon of salt, 3 cups of bread flour, and 1 teaspoon of yeast.

Snap the pan into the machine and close the lid. Add 1/2 cup of raisins in the automatic fruit and nut dispenser. Plug the unit into an outlet. Choose the Sweet setting and your preferred color of the crust. Press the Start/Stop button. Once the unit is done with the cooking, carefully remove the pan and transfer the loaf to a wire rack to cool.

Pumpkin Bread with Pecan

Here are the steps to follow to make 1 1/2-pound loaf bread: Put 1 egg in the measuring cup. Make sure that it is at room temperature. Add enough water with the temperature of 80 to 90 degrees Fahrenheit to the cup to measure 3/4 cup along with the egg.

Place them into the bread pan and add the other ingredients in this exact order: 1/3 cup of cooked pumpkin, 1 1/2 teaspoons of vanilla extract, 3 tablespoons of unsalted butter cut into cubes, 3 tablespoons of light brown sugar, 2 teaspoons of dried orange peel, a teaspoon of ground cinnamon, 1 1/2 teaspoons of salt, 1/4 teaspoon of ground nutmeg, 3 1/2 cups of bread flour, and 1 1/2 teaspoons of yeast.

Place the pan inside the unit and close the lid. Put half a cup of toasted pecans in the automatic fruit and nut dispenser. Plug the unit and choose the Sweet setting and your chosen crust color. Press the Start/Stop button. Once the cooking process is done, remove the pan and unmold the loaf onto a wire rack to cool.

Panettone

To make 1 1/2-pound loaf bread, measure the ingredients into the pan in this exact order: 1 egg at room temperature, 1/2 cup of milk with the temperature of 80 to 90 degrees Fahrenheit, 1/4 cup of unsalted butter cut into cubes, 1/4 cup of sugar, 1/4 cup of chopped candied mix fruits, 1/4 cup of chopped candied cherries, 2 tablespoons of chopped candied lemon peel, 1 teaspoon of dried orange peel, half a teaspoon of anise seed, 3/4 teaspoon of salt, 2 3/4 cups of bread flour, and 2 teaspoons of yeast.

Snap the pan into the unit and lock the lid. Add 1/3 cup of lightly toasted pine nuts in the automatic fruit and nut dispenser. Plug the unit and select Sweet setting and your chosen color of the crust. Press the Start/Stop button. Once done, remove the pan and unmold the bread. Place it on a wire rack to cool.

5 - Conclusion

After trying out the recipes and using the bread machine several times, you will get an idea of what works for you and how you can tweak the measurement to achieve your preferred texture of the bread. To ensure success in all your tries, always use fresh ingredients, especially for the flour and yeast. The bread will fail to rise if the yeast has been stored for a long time.

In adding the ingredients, put all the liquid items first, followed by the dry items. Make a small hole in the middle of the ingredients where you will place the yeast before putting the bread pan into the unit.

Most of the bread machines come with troubleshooting tips so that you would know what to do in case you encounter certain problems while using one. Enjoy this handy process of bread making and in due time, you'll be able to whip up your own recipes to make new flavors of bread to suit your taste.

Thank You

As we reach the end of this book, I want to say thanks for reading this book.

I want to get this information out to as many people as possible. If you found this book helpful, I would greatly appreciate you leaving me a review. This helps others find the book as well.

Disclaimer

This document is geared towards providing exact and reliable information in regards to the topic and issue covered. The publication is sold on the idea that the publisher is not required to render an accounting, officially permitted, or otherwise, qualified services. If advice is necessary, legal, financial, medical or professional, a practiced individual in the profession should be ordered.

This information is not presented by a financial or medical practitioner and is for entertainment, educational and informational purposes only. The content is not intended as a substitute for professional medical advice, diagnosis, or treatment. Always seek the advice of your physician or other qualified health care provider with any questions you may have regarding a medical condition. Never disregard professional medical advice or delay in seeking it because of something you have read.

The information provided herein is stated to be truthful and consistent, in that any liability, in terms of inattention or otherwise, by any usage or abuse of any policies, processes, or directions contained within is the solitary and utter responsibility of the recipient reader. Under no circumstances will any legal responsibility or blame be held against the

DISCLAIMER

publisher for any reparation, damages, or monetary loss
due to the information herein, either directly or indirectly.

Last Updated: 10.Jul.2018

www.ingramcontent.com/pod-product-compliance
Lightning Source LLC
LaVergne TN
LVHW010707200726
843507LV00011B/2052